d e f

k l m

q r s t

x y z

For Claudia

First published 1997 by Walker Books Ltd
87 Vauxhall Walk, London SE11 5HJ

10 9 8 7 6 5 4 3 2 1

This book has been typeset
in New Baskerville Educational.

Printed in Hong Kong

British Library Cataloguing
in Publication Data
A catalogue record for this book
is available from the British Library.

ISBN 0-7445-4413-0

Flora McDonnell's

A B C

WALKER BOOKS
AND SUBSIDIARIES
LONDON • BOSTON • SYDNEY

Aa

ants

ALLIGATOR

butterfly

B b

BEAR

cats

Cc

CAR

Dd

DINOSAURS

duck

ELEPHANT   egg

E e   egg

Ff FLAMINGO

fish

Gg glove

GIANT

HIPPOPOTAMUS

hare

Hh

I i

ice-cream

IBIS

jellybeans

J j

JUGGLER

Kk

kite

KING

L l

ladybird

LEMON

MOON

Mm

mouse

Nn

newts

THE NEWTSPAPER

NEWSPAPER

ORANG-UTAN

orange

Oo

P p

PIG

pea

Qq

quails

QUEEN

Rr

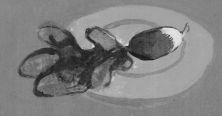 radish

RHINOCEROS

star

S s

SHIP

T t

TIGER

teapot

U u

umbrella

UNICORN

VOLCANO

vulture

Vv

WHALE

W w

watering-can

X-RAY FISH

X x

x-ray fish

Yy

yo-yo

YAK

ZEBRA

Z z

z z z z z z z z z z z z

zip

A   B   C

G   H   I   J

N   O   P

U   V   W